Songs of Joy
and others

By
William H. Davies

London
A. C. Fifield, 13 Clifford's Inn, E.C
1911

PRINTED BY
WILLIAM BRENDON AND SON, LTD.
PLYMOUTH

Some of these poems have appeared in *The Nation*, *The English Review*, *The Westminster Gazette*, and *The Vineyard*. The author thanks the editors for permission to reprint them.

Contents

Songs of Joy

SING out, my Soul, thy songs of joy;
    Such as a happy bird will sing
Beneath a Rainbow's lovely arch
    In early spring.

Think not of Death in thy young days;
    Why shouldst thou that grim tyrant fear,
And fear him not when thou art old,
    And he is near.

Strive not for gold, for greedy fools
    Measure themselves by poor men never;
Their standard still being richer men,
    Makes them poor ever.

Train up thy mind to feel content,
    What matters then how low thy store;
What we enjoy, and not possess,
    Makes rich or poor.

Filled with sweet thought, then happy I
  Take not my state from others' eyes;
What's in my mind—not on my flesh
  Or theirs—I prize.

Sing, happy Soul, thy songs of joy;
  Such as a Brook sings in the wood,
That all night has been strengthened by
  Heaven's purer flood.

The Example

HERE'S an example from
    A Butterfly;
That on a rough, hard rock
    Happy can lie;
Friendless and all alone
On this unsweetened stone.

Now let my bed be hard,
    No care take I;
I'll make my joy like this
    Small Butterfly;
Whose happy heart has power
To make a stone a flower.

In May

In May

YES, I will spend the livelong day
    With Nature in this month of May;
And sit beneath the trees, and share
My bread with birds whose homes are there;
While cows lie down to eat, and sheep
Stand to their necks in grass so deep;
While birds do sing with all their might,
As though they felt the earth in flight.
This is the hour I dreamed of, when
I sat surrounded by poor men;
And thought of how the Arab sat
Alone at evening, gazing at
The stars that bubbled in clear skies;

And of young dreamers, when their eyes
Enjoyed methought a precious boon
In the adventures of the Moon
Whose light, behind the Clouds' dark bars,
Searched for her stolen flocks of stars.

In May

When I, hemmed in by wrecks of men,
Thought of some lonely cottage then,
Full of sweet books; and miles of sea,
With passing ships, in front of me;
And having, on the other hand,
A flowery, green, bird-singing land.

The Flood

The Flood

I THOUGHT my true love slept;
　Behind her chair I crept
And pulled out a long pin;
The golden flood came out,
She shook it all about,
　With both our faces in.

Ah! little wren, I know
Your mossy, small nest now
　A windy, cold place is;
No eye can see my face,
Howe'er it watch the place
　Where I half drown in bliss.

When I am drowned half dead,
She laughs and shakes her head;
　Flogged by her hair-waves, I
Withdraw my face from there;
But never once, I swear,
　She heard a mercy-cry.

Leisure

WHAT is this life if, full of care,
    We have no time to stand and stare.

No time to stand beneath the boughs
And stare as long as sheep or cows.

No time to see, when woods we pass,
Where squirrels hide their nuts in grass.

No time to see, in broad daylight,
Streams full of stars, like skies at night.

No time to turn at Beauty's glance,
And watch her feet, how they can dance.

No time to wait till her mouth can
Enrich that smile her eyes began.

A poor life this if, full of care,
We have no time to stand and stare.

Love's Power

I ASK not of high tide or low,
   That ships may out of port or in;
When thou dost come, and not before,
   Commerce doth on my mind begin.

Until I see thee come like spring,
   My spirits' streams are locked in ice;
But navigation opens, Love,
   As soon as I can hear thy voice.

Thy touch can launch a fleet of boats
   Sunk to their decks with bales of bliss,
To take the tide of my blood-veins
   Straight to my Heart's Metropolis.

Fancy's Home

TELL me, Fancy, sweetest child,
　　Of thy parents and thy birth ;
Had they silk, and had they gold,
　　And a park to wander forth,
With a castle green and old ?

In a cottage I was born,
　　My kind father was Content,
My dear mother Innocence ;
　　On wild fruits of wonderment
I have nourished ever since.

War

YE Liberals and Conservatives,
　　Have pity on our human lives,
　Waste no more blood on human strife;
Until we know some way to use
This human blood we take or lose,
　　'Tis sin to sacrifice our life.

When pigs are stuck we save their blood
And make black puddings for our food,
　　The sweetest and the cheapest meat;
And many a woman, man and boy
Have ate those puddings with great joy,
　　And oft-times in the open street.

Let's not have war till we can make,
Of this sweet life we lose or take,
　　Some kind of pudding of man's gore;
So that the clergy in each parish,
May save the lives of those that famish
　　Because meat's dear and times are poor.

Self-Love

SHE had two eyes as blue as Heaven,
    Ten times as warm they shone;
And yet her heart was hard and cold
    As any shell or stone.

Her mouth was like a soft red rose
    When Phœbus drinks its dew;
But oh, that cruel thorn inside
    Pierced many a fond heart true.

She had a step that walked unheard,
    It made the stones like grass;
Yet that light step has crushed a heart,
    As light as that step was.

Those glowing eyes, those smiling lips,
    I have lived now to prove,
Were not for you, were not for me,
    But came of her self-love.

Yet, like a cow for acorns that
    Have made it suffer pain,
So, though her charms are poisonous,
    I moan for them again.

In the Wood

I LIE on Joy's enchanted ground :
　　No other noise but these green trees
　　That sigh and cling to every breeze ;
And that deep solemn, hollow sound
　　Born of the grave, and made by Bees.

Now do I think of this packed world,
　　Where thousands of rich people sweat,
　　Like common slaves, in idle fret ;
Not knowing how to buy with gold
　　This house of Joy, that makes no debt.

What little wealth true Joy doth need !
　　I pay for wants that make no show ;　·
　　I pay my way and nothing owe ;
I drink my ale, I smoke my weed,
　　And take my time where'er I go.

Sheep

WHEN I was once in Baltimore,
    A man came up to me and cried,
"Come, I have eighteen hundred sheep,
    And we will sail on Tuesday's tide.

"If you will sail with me, young man,
    I'll pay you fifty shillings down;
These eighteen hundred sheep I take
    From Baltimore to Glasgow town."

He paid me fifty shillings down,
    I sailed with eighteen hundred sheep;
We soon had cleared the harbour's mouth,
    We soon were in the salt sea deep.

The first night we were out at sea
    Those sheep were quiet in their mind;
The second night they cried with fear—
    They smelt no pastures in the wind.

They sniffed, poor things, for their green fields,
    They cried so loud I could not sleep:
For fifty thousand shillings down
    I would not sail again with sheep.

Love and Immortality

MY wonder is the great bright sun,
   Beneath whose looks we live and die;
Whose strong bright arm of light can lift
  The water into the Heavens high;
I marvel too at beauty's power
In flesh and rock, in tree and flower.

And yet, in spite of these fine things,
  I have no hope in life to come—
Save that my spirit, like my flesh,
  Will find in common grass a home;
I have no hope of life at last
Outshining this when it is past.

Love, only Love, can change my mind;
  I for that passion great will claim
Immunity from time and space,
  From floods of water and of flame;
A perfect immortality
Must qualify that love in me.

Days that have been

CAN I forget the sweet days that have been,
  When poetry first began to warm my blood;
When from the hills of Gwent I saw the earth
  Burned into two by Severn's silver flood:

When I would go alone at night to see
  The moonlight, like a big white butterfly,
Dreaming on that old castle near Caerleon,
  While at its side the Usk went softly by:

When I would stare at lovely clouds in Heaven,
  Or watch them when reported by deep streams;
When feeling pressed like thunder, but would not
  Break into that grand music of my dreams.

Can I forget the sweet days that have been,
  The villages so green I have been in;
Llantarnam, Magor, Malpas, and Llanwern,
  Liswery, old Caerleon, and Alteryn?

24   Days that have been

Can I forget the banks of Malpas Brook,
   Or Ebbw's voice in such a wild delight,
As on he dashed with pebbles in his throat,
   Gurgling towards the sea with all his might?

Ah, when I see a leafy village now,
   I sigh and ask it for Llantarnam's green;
I ask each river where is Ebbw's voice—
   In memory of the sweet days that have been.

To a Working Man

YOU working man, of what avail
  Are these fine teachings of the great,
  To raise you to a better state;
When you forget in pots of ale
  That slavery's not your common fate.

You victim to all fraud and greed,
  Shun now that mind-destroying state:
  Go, meet your masters in debate:
Go home from work and think and read—
  To make our laws is your true fate.

Treasures

HE hailed me with a cheerful voice,
    I answered him with ready lips;
As though we sailed the briny seas,
    And hailed from passing ships.

"Come in," quoth he, "and I will show
    Thee treasures few men saw before."
He from his pocket took a key
    And opened wide his door.

He seemed no more than other men,
    His voice was calm, his eyes were cold;
He was not tall, he was not short,
    Nor seemed he young nor old.

I'll see some treasures now, methought—
    Some work in silk and ivory;
Some painted trays and vases quaint,
    Things with a history.

I saw at once some glittering beads
  That seemed like berries fit to eat;
Such as make children leave the woods
  Crying for their home sweet.

" Aye, aye," quoth he, " a little maid
  Played with them fifty years ago;
She's perished on the scaffold since—
  That's why I prize them so.

" Pray sit thee down in comfort now,
  For I have treasures rich and rare."
He went upstairs, I sat me down
  And round the room did stare.

That room looked strange; a little fire,
  The lamp burned low, the hour was late;
A horse outside cropped grass—the sound
  Seemed like the steps of Fate.

The furniture in that man's room
  Seemed part of one large, deadly plant
Which if I touched would hold me fast,
  To perish soon of want.

Aye, I confess, I trembling stayed,
  Thralled by an unexplained desire;
I shook like negro in his hut,
  Sick at a little fire.

I heard him tumbling things about,
  Methought I heard a murder call
And blows; and then the blows did cease-
  I heard a body fall.

Then all was still, how still it was!
  I heard him breathing hard; at last
I heard him with a load caught in
  The narrow stairway fast.

And now he shows his face again;
  I see a bundle on his arm,
'A dress, a sheet, a boot—and things
  Too simple to alarm.

"Now list," quoth he, "I told thee once
  That I had treasures rich and rare:
This sheet did smother a small babe,
  It was a baron's heir.

" This long, black dress a poisoner wore—
 Her head was chopped off with an axe ;
'Tis priceless unto those that made
 Her figure show in wax.

" This is the boot, one of a pair,
 The other matters not "—he said ;
" 'Twas with this boot a murderer kicked
 To bits his dead man's head.

" These bones were found upon a raft,
 And brought to shore by seamen true :
Bones of a little boy, picked clean
 By a cannibal crew.

" When Bill Black murdered Liza Green,
 As she sat down to pickled pork,
He finished her sweet supper with
 This very knife and fork.

" This scarf, which ties them all in one,
 Was my own father's, he one day
Hanged himself to a beam by it—
 I've other things, so prithee stay."

30 Treasures

He whistling went upstairs again,
   I softly crept towards the door
And vanished in the night, nor saw,
   Nor wished to see him more.

Beauty's Revenge

PROUD Margery rang her peal of bells ;
    " If you despise all womankind,
Take care, young man," she said, " take care
    No woman ever plagues your mind "—
The young man smoothed his own soft hair.

And how it came about, who knows,
    It is for womankind to tell ;
Before a full-blown rose could fade,
    That man was suffering passion's hell
For Margery, that merry maid.

She brought ripe cherries to his sleep,
    Her teeth and eyes they shone at night ;
" I am," he murmured in his dreams,
    " A poor black ruin blessed with light—
From Margery come those heavenly beams."

He dreamt he saw her hair at hand ;
  "My soul," he sighed, "is little worth,
My life till now had little hope,
  But I will find my heaven on earth
By holding to this silken rope."

He told his love to Margery soon,
  She bird-like cocked her cruel head,
She rang her peal of bells again :
  "Nay, I despise you men," she said—
" Good-bye, young man, and take no pain."

Days too Short

WHEN primroses are out in Spring,
 And small, blue violets come between;
 When merry birds sing on boughs green,
And rills, as soon as born, must sing;

When butterflies will make side-leaps,
 As though escaped from Nature's hand
 Ere perfect quite; and bees will stand
Upon their heads in fragrant deeps;

When small clouds are so silvery white
 Each seems a broken rimmèd moon—
 When such things are, this world too soon,
For me, doth wear the veil of Night.

Dreaming of Death

WHEN I, awake, have thoughts of Death,
Two friends can ease me of my grief :
First comes Philosophy, who says,
"Fear brings Death soon, and Life is brief;"
Then comes Old Age with looks so calm,
In spite of Death, and he so near,
That when I see his happy face,
It banishes my fear.

But when in sleep I dream of Death,
Fear cuts me then with a sharp knife :
The Death that comes to me in dreams,
Is but to feel a stronger life ;
For only my poor body dies,
My mind is still to this life bound ;
I hear the merry world go by,
But cannot make a sound.

The Stars at Work

I SEE the busy stars at work,
    And question what they do
There comes a voice—" They knit a shroud,
    A dead man's shroud for you."

" No, no," a second voice doth say,
    " I'll tell thee what they make :
They knit a veil a lady'll wear
    Some morning for your sake."

Yours is the knowledge, lady, speak ;
    The truth is known to thee ;
Is it a shroud or bridal veil,
    Death or sweet life for me ?

The Temper of a Maid

THE Swallow dives in yonder air,
   The Robin sings with sweetest ease,
The Apple shines among the leaves,
The Leaf is dancing in the breeze;
The Butterfly's on a warm stone,
The Bee is suckled by a flower;
The Wasp's inside a ripe red plum,
The Ant has found his load this hour;
The Squirrel counts and hides his nuts,
The Stoat is on a scent that burns;
The Mouse is nibbling a young shoot,
The Rabbit sits beside his ferns;
The Snake has found a sunny spot,
The Frog and Snail a slimy shade;
But I can find no joy on earth,
All through the temper of a maid.

The Power of Music

O THOSE sweet notes, so soft and faint; that
  seemed
  Locked up inside a thick walled house of stone;
And then that sudden rush of sound, as though
  The doors and windows were wide-open thrown.

Do with me, O sweet music, as thou wilt,
  I am thy slave to either laugh or weep;
Thy power can make thy slave a lover proud,
  Or friendless man that has no place to sleep.

I hear thy gentle whisper and again
  Hear ripples lap the quays of sheltered docks;
I hear thy thunder and it brings to mind
  Dark Colorado scaling his huge rocks.

I hear thy joyous cries and think of birds
  Delirious when the sun doth rise in May;
I hear thy moans and think me of poor cows
  That miss at night the calves they licked by day.

I hear thee wail and think of that sad queen
    Who saw her lover's disappearing mast;
How she, who drank and wasted a rich pearl—
    To prove her love—was left to wail at last.

Do with me, O sweet Music, as thou wilt;
    Till even thou art robbed by jealous Sleep
Of those sweet senses thou hast forced from me—
    And I can neither laugh with thee nor weep.

Christ the Man

LORD, I say nothing; I profess
    No faith in thee nor Christ thy Son :
Yet no man ever heard me mock
    A true believing one.

If knowledge is not great enough
    To give a man believing power,
Lord, he must wait in thy great hand
    Till revelation's hour.

Meanwhile he'll follow Christ the man,
    In that humanity he taught,
Which to the poor and the oppressed,
    Gives its best time and thought.

Ingratitude

Ingratitude

AM I a fool?
    So let it be,
For half the world
    Will pity me.

Ingratitude
    Is not my name;
Thieves, called by that,
    Are dumb for shame.

A fool—the world
    Will pity me;
Ungrateful—let
    No mercy be.

The Grey-haired Child

THY father was a drunken man,
    He threatened thee with a sharp knife;
And thou, a child not ten years old,
    Lay trembling for thy life.

Lay trembling in the dark all night,
    Sleep could not seal thine eye or ear;
Thy hair, which was a dark rich brown,
    Is now made grey by fear.

The Posts

A YEAR'S a post, on which
    It saith
The distance—growing less—
    To Death.

Some posts I missed, beguiled
    By Song
And Beauty, as I passed
    Along.

But sad am I to think
    This day
Of forty posts passed on
    My way.

For not one post I now
    Must pass
Will 'scape these eyes of mine,
    Alas!

Rich or Poor

WITH thy true love I have more wealth
    Than Charon's piled-up bank doth hold ;
Where he makes kings lay down their crowns
    And lifelong misers leave their gold.

Without thy love I've no more wealth
    Than seen upon that other shore ;
That cold, bare bank he rows them to—
    Those kings and misers made so poor.

The Harvest Home

THE Harvest Home's a home indeed;
    If my lord bishop drank ale there,
He'd want to kiss the beggar wench,
    And change his gown with her, I swear.

The Harvest Home's a place to love,
    These is no better boose on sale;
Angels in Heaven—I take my oath—
    Can find no better glass of ale.

There's courage in such boose as that:
    Old Dicky drank but one small mug,
And then, to please the harvest girls,
    Said, " Look ! " and swallowed a live frog.

The landlord draws to suit my taste,
    I never knew his wife to fail;
But, somehow, what the daughter draws
    Is—by my soul and body—Ale !

The Winged Flower

BRIGHT Butterfly,
  Dreaming with thy
Wings spread lengthways;
Full of black eyes,
And black bars rolled
Across red gold,
Straight from thy lips
To wings' white tips:
Wert thou a flower,
Until some power
Made thee to fly—
Then, ere we die,
Oh, let me know
Where such flowers grow.
Lead where they lie,
Now, lovely Fly.
On this leaf wet,
Dreaming worlds yet
Greener than ours—
Show me those flowers
Just when they rise
Live Butterflies.

Seeking Beauty

COLD winds can never freeze, nor thunder sour
    The cup of cheer that Beauty draws for me
Out of those azure Heavens and this green Earth—
   I drink and drink, and thirst the more I see.

To see the dewdrops thrill the blades of grass,
    Makes my whole body shake; for here's my
      choice
Of either sun or shade, and both are green—
    A Chaffinch laughs in his melodious voice.

The banks are stormed by Speedwell, that blue
    flower
    So like a little Heaven with one star out;
I see an amber lake of Buttercups,
    And Hawthorn foams the hedges round about.

The old Oak tree looks now so green and young,
    That even Swallows perch awhile and sing:
This is that time of year, so sweet and warm,
    When Bats wait not for Stars ere they take wing.

Seeking Beauty

As long as I love Beauty I am young,
  Am young or old as I love more or less ;
When Beauty is not heeded or seems stale,
  My life's a cheat, let Death end my distress.

The Owl

THE boding Owl, that in despair
    Doth moan and shiver on warm nights-
Shall that bird prophecy for me
    The fall of Heaven's eternal lights?

When in the thistled field of Age
    I take my final walk on earth
Still will I make that Owl's despair
    A thing to fill my heart with mirth.

The Little Man

LAST night I sat in thought,
   When, near my bended head,
I saw a little man,
   And this is what he said :
" Of all the eyes and ears
   That in this great world be,
There's not one eye or ear
   Takes any note of thee."

" Peace, hold thy froward tongue,
   Thou mocking Imp," said I ;
" Joy, that is man's true aim,
   Until the hour we die ;
A dream that gives us joy,
   Though vain, is our sweet friend :
Man's *deeds* are but vain dreams
   That soon must have an end."

Sound and Grace

MY love laughs sweeter than a brook
　　That has been drinking rain all day;
She like a blackbird sings, when he
　　Has not one feather dry, in May.

When I can hear her laugh like that,
　　My hand starts forth to clutch her gown;
Lord, if she dances while she laughs,
　　My mind makes plans to pull her down.

A Mother's Science

I HEARD a man once say this world
 Was but a speck in space;
A leaf upon a shoreless tide,
 That had no resting-place.

I told him then how vast this world
 Was to my own poor mind;
Of all the places seen, and still
 My child I could not find.

I told that man where I had been,
 I mentioned towns around;
And still my boy, in all these years,
 Is never to be found.

The East in Gold

SOMEHOW this world is wonderful at times,
  As it has been from early morn in May ;
Since first I heard the cock-a-doodle-do—
  Timekeeper on green farms—at break of day.

Soon after that I heard ten thousand birds,
  Which made me think an angel brought a bin
Of golden grain, and none was scattered yet—
  To rouse those birds to make that merry din.

I could not sleep again, for such wild cries,
  And went out early into their green world;
And then I saw what set their little tongues
  To scream for joy—they saw the East in gold.

Man

I SAW Time running by—
   Stop, Thief! was all the cry.
I heard a voice say, Peace!
Let this vain clamour cease.
Can ye bring lightning back
That leaves upon its track
Men, horses, oak trees dead?
Canst bring back Time? it said.
There's nothing in Man's mind
Can catch Time up behind;
In front of that fast Thief
There's no one—end this grief.
Tut, what is Man? How frail!
A grain, a little nail,
The wind, a change of cloth—
A fly can give him death.
Some fishes in the sea
Are born to outlive thee,
And owls, and toads, and trees—
And is Man more than these?

54 Man

I see Man's face in all
Things, be they great or small;
I see the face of him
In things that fly or swim;
One fate for all, I see—
Whatever that may be.
Imagination fits
Life to a day; though its
Length were a thousand years,
'Twould not decrease our fears;
What strikes men cold and dumb
Is that Death's time *must* come.

Sadness and Joy

I PRAY you, Sadness, leave me soon,
　In sweet invention thou art poor !
Thy sister Joy can make ten songs
　While thou art making four.

One hour with thee is sweet enough ;
　But when we find the whole day gone
And no created thing is left—
　We mourn the evil done.

Thou art too slow to shape thy thoughts
　In stone, on canvas, or in song ;
But Joy, being full of active heat,
　Must do some deed ere long.

Thy sighs are gentle, sweet thy tears ;
　But if thou canst not help a man
To prove in substance what he feels—
　Then give me Joy, who can.

56 Sadness and Joy

Therefore, sweet Sadness, leave me soon,
Let thy bright sister Joy come more ;
For she can make ten lovely songs
While thou art making four.

Love's Happiness

BLOW, blow, thou Eastern wind,
    Since Love can draw thy sting;
The South blows to my mind,
    And does sweet odours bring—
If only Love is kind.

Spout, spout, you frowning cloud,
    Since Love cares not for rain:
With every spout allowed,
    You beat on me in vain—
As though I wore Death's shroud.

Rumble, you thunderstorm,
    Since Love's voice cannot fail
To sing more loud and warm—
    Like a fine nightingale
Paced by your angry storm.

Love's Happiness

Then thunder, cloud, or wind,
  Come either, stay or go;
If Love to me is kind,
  Rumble, or rain, or blow
Comes easy to my mind.

Circumstance

DOWN in the deep salt sea
        A mighty fish will make
Its own strong current, which
    The little ones must take ;
Which they must follow still,
No matter for their will.

Here, in this human sea,
    Is Circumstance, that takes
Men where they're loth to go ;
    It fits them false and makes
Machines of master souls,
And masters of dull fools.

Slum Children

YOUR songs at night a drunkard sings,
    Stones, sticks and rags your daily
        flowers;
Like fishes' lips, a bluey white,
    Such lips, poor mites, are yours.

Poor little things, so sad and solemn,
    Whose lives are passed in human crowds—
When in the water I can see
    Heaven with a flock of clouds.

Poor little mites that breathe foul air,
    Where garbage chokes the sink and drain—
Now when the hawthorn smells so sweet,
    Wet with the summer rain.

But few of ye will live for long;
    Ye are but small new islands seen,
To disappear before your lives
    Can grow and be made green.

To a Rich Lady

THOUGH thou hast silk to wear, and though
    Thou'rt clad in it from head to toe—
Still in your hair, that soft warm nest,
My mind would hatch its thoughts and rest.

Though thou hast gems as well, and though
They brighter than the dewdrops glow—
Still would I take my full supplies
Of warmth and light from those two eyes.

Though thou hast cars to drive, and though
Thou'rt driven as the winds that blow—
Still would I find a greater pleasure
To see thee walk an easy measure.

Though thou hast rooms to spare, and though
More than friends need, that come and go—
Still would I ask for no more space
Than where two bodies could embrace.

To Sparrows Fighting

STOP, feathered bullies !
    Peace, angry birds ;
You common Sparrows that,
   For a few words,
Roll fighting in wet mud,
To shed each other's blood.

Look at those Linnets, they
   Like ladies sing ;
See how those Swallows, too,
   Play on the wing ;
All other birds close by
Are gentle, clean and shy.

And yet maybe your life's
   As sweet as theirs ;
The common poor that fight
   Live not for years
In one long frozen state
Of anger, like the great.

A Woman's Glory

A WOMAN'S glory is not hair,
  It is her voice so soft and sweet;
Her hair can be what'er she wills,
  Her voice will stand no counterfeit;
So let her sing, and laugh in tones
Of water caught by rocks and stones.

When woman works from home or drinks,
  And has no time or love to charm
Her young with song between their meals,
  The world and they must suffer harm:
They'll stone dumb creatures, and they'll yell
Around the blind like imps from hell.

The Happy Child

The Happy Child

I SAW this day sweet flowers grow thick—
   But not one like the child did pick.

I heard the packhounds in green park—
But no dog like the child heard bark.

I heard this day bird after bird—
But not one like the child has heard.

A hundred butterflies saw I—
But not one like the child saw fly.

I saw the horses roll in grass—
But no horse like the child saw pass.

My world this day has lovely been—
But not like what the child has seen.

The Two Flocks

WHERE are you going to now, white sheep,
    Walking the green hill-side ;
To join that whiter flock on top,
  And share their pride ?

Stay where you are, you silly sheep :
  When you arrive up there,
You'll find that whiter flock on top
  Clouds in the air !

A Dream

I MET her in the leafy woods,
  Early a Summer's night;
I saw her white teeth in the dark,
  There was no better light.

Had she not come up close and made
  Those lilies their light spread,
I had not proved her mouth a rose,
  So round, so fresh, so red.

Her voice was gentle, soft and sweet,
  In words she was not strong;
Yet her low twitter had more charm
  Than any full-mouthed song.

We walked in silence to her cave,
  With but few words to say;
But ever and anon she stopped
  For kisses on the way

A Dream

And after every burning kiss
　　She laughed and danced around;
Back-bending, with her breasts straight up,
　　Her hair it touched the ground.

When we lay down, she held me fast,
　　She held me like a leech;
Ho, ho! I know what her red tongue
　　Is made for, if not speech.

Into my mouth it goes with mine,
　　I felt its soft warm waves;
That fair Enchantress knew full well
　　The way to make men slaves.

And what is this, how strange, how sweet!
　　Her teeth are made to bite
The man she gives her passion to,
　　And not to boast their white.

O night of joy! O morning's grief!
　　For when, with passion done,
Rocked on her breast I fell asleep,
　　I woke, and lay alone.

The Elements

NO house of stone
    Was built for me;
When the Sun shines—
    I am a bee.

No sooner comes
    The Rain so warm,
I come to light—
    I am a worm.

When the Winds blow,
    I do not strip,
But set my sails—
    I am a ship.

When Lightning comes,
    It plays with me
And I with it—
    I am a tree.

When drowned men rise
  At Thunder's word,
Sings Nightingale—
  I am a bird.

Beauty's Bait

WHEN Beauty scents with love her bait,
     What artful secrets meet their fate;
What things we darkly hide with care,
Leap out before we are aware.

Thinking of girls in flesh and blood,
And not of any shadowy brood—
What poor tame sport will Beauty find
When I confess to her my mind.

When I shall tell of girls whose looks
Came out of painted cloth or books,
Then Beauty, erstwhile full of thought,
Must laugh when such poor things are caught.

The Heap of Rags

ONE night when I went down
    Thames' side, in London Town,
A heap of rags saw I,
And sat me down close by.
That thing could shout and bawl,
But showed no face at all;
When any steamer passed
And blew a loud shrill blast,
That heap of rags would sit
And make a sound like it;
When struck the clock's deep bell,
It made those peals as well.
When winds did moan around,
It mocked them with that sound;
When all was quiet, it
Fell into a strange fit;
Would sigh, and moan and roar,
It laughed, and blessed, and swore.
Yet that poor thing, I know,
Had neither friend nor foe;

The Heap of Rags

Its blessing or its curse
Made no one better or worse.
I left it in that place—
The thing that showed no face,
Was it a man that had
Suffered till he went mad?
So many showers and not
One rainbow in the lot;
Too many bitter fears
To make a pearl from tears.

The Quarrel

HEAR me, thou proud, deceitful maid,
 Tell how thy charms must droop and fade;
Long ere thy days are done, thou'lt be
Alive for Memory's mockery.
Soft flesh will soon hang hard and dry
Like seaweed on the rocks; that eye
Soon lose its clearness, like a flood
Where late the drinking cows have stood.
Thy berry-lips, now full and red,
Will dry and crack, like snakeskins shed;
And those white stones they keep inside,
Will blacken, break, and then you'll hide.
That hair which like a golden net
Hangs loose and free, a trap well set
To catch my silly fingers now—
Will soon cause thee much grief to show.
Thy voice, now like a flawless bell,
Which thou dost ring so sweet and well—
Will shame thee into silence soon.
Thy form, tied like a silk balloon,

74 The Quarrel

Full of sweet gas, straining to rise
From common earth, and sail those skies—
Will sit all huddled in a chair,
Cold at a fire, and springtime there.
These things I told a maid one day,
And laughed with scorn, and went my way;
I laughed with scorn, as home I stept—
Ah, but all night I sighed and wept.

O Happy Blackbird

O HAPPY Blackbird, happy soul,
  I hear in song's delirium now :
Thou dost forget the days just past,
  Of cold and hunger in the snow.

Would that man's memory were the same ;
  For he, alas ! must backward cast
His misery-fearing eyes and fill
  The future with his troubles past.

Thou hast no gift of Hope, like man,
  To ease thee of a present pain ;
But where's a man, in all this world,
  Who would not sacrifice that gain,
O happy Blackbird : for the power
  To use like thee his present hour.

To a Bore

I WALK to look,
   To think, and feel
Things that to you
   Make no appeal.

Wert thou the same—
   More joy for thee
To walk without
   My company.

But now—a fool
   Walks out with thee,
As sure as one
   Walks out with me.

Fairies, Take Care

A THOUSAND blessings, Puck, on you
For knotting that long grass which threw
Into my arms a maid; for we
Have told our love and kissed, and she
Will lie a-bed in a sweet fright.
So, all ye Fairies who to-night
May take that stormy passage where
Her bosom's quicksands are, take care
Of whirlpools too: beware all you
Of that great tempest Love must brew.
The waves will rock your breath near out;
First sunk, then tossed and rolled about,
Now on your heads, now on your feet—
You'll be near swamped and, for life sweet,
Be glad to cross that stormy main,
And stand on something firm again.
Would I could see her while she sleeps,
And smiles to feel you climb those steeps,
Where you at last will stand up clear
Upon their cherry tops, and cheer.

78   Fairies, Take Care

And that ye are not lost, take care,
In that deep forest of her hair :
Yet ye may enter naked stark,
It gets more warm as it gets dark.
So, Fairies, fear not any harm,
While in those woods so dark and warm

Captives

IN this deep hollow, lying down,
　　I, looking up at Heaven, can see
You pretty little clouds shut in
　　By green hills all around—like me.

And all you simple, little clouds
　　Seem glad at my captivity :
Without a thought that I can smile
　　As much at you as you at me.

The Doubtful One

The Doubtful One

WHEN tigers flee from fire, the deer
    Have nothing but that fire to fear ;
So, driven by Love's flames I see
No danger save thy cruelty.

Let not thy breast, to which I fly
For pity's milk, be hard and dry :
Let not thy heart, to which I come,
Refuse my homeless life a home.

Now, wrecked and cuffed by many a sea,
I swim for safety unto thee ;
Let not sharp rocks that poor wretch cut.
Who for his life clings hand and foot.

The Little Ones

THE little ones are put in bed,
    And both are laughing, lying down;
Their father, and their mother too,
    Are gone on Christmas-eve to town.

"Old Santa Claus will bring a horse,
    Gee up:" cried little Will, with glee;
"If I am good, I'll have a doll
    From Santa Claus"—laughed Emily.

The little ones are gone to sleep,
    Their father and their mother now
Are coming home, with many more—
    They're drunk, and make a merry row.

The little ones on Christmas morn
    Jump up, like skylarks from the grass;
And then they stand as still as stones,
    And just as cold as stones, Alas!

The Little Ones

No horse, no doll beside their bed,
　No sadder little ones could be ;
" We did some wrong," said little Will—
　" We must have sinned," sobbed Emily.

Shopping

WHEN thou hast emptied thy soft purse,
    Take not from men more merchandise:
Full well I know they'd trust thy looks,
And enter no accounts in books,
    Of goods bought by thy lovely eyes.

Take not advantage of that hand,
    That men, admiring it too much,
Forget the value of their stuff,
And think that empty hand enough—
    To make poor bankrupt men of such.

Let not that voice of thine, like silk
    Translated into sound, commend
Plain cloth to Jews, lest they should raise
The price of it to match thy praise,
    And the poor suffer in the end.

The Sleepers

A S I walked down the waterside
   This silent morning, wet and dark;
Before the cocks in farmyards crowed,
   Before the dogs began to bark;
Before the hour of five was struck
By old Westminster's mighty clock:

As I walked down the waterside
   This morning, in the cold damp air,
I saw a hundred women and men
   Huddled in rags and sleeping there:
These people have no work, thought I,
And long before their time they die.

That moment, on the waterside,
   A lighted car came at a bound;
I looked inside, and saw a score
   Of pale and weary men that frowned;
Each man sat in a huddled heap,

The Sleepers

Ten cars rushed down the waterside,
   Like lighted coffins in the dark;
With twenty dead men in each car,
   That must be brought alive by work:
These people work too hard, thought I,
And long before their time they die.

The Bed-sitting-room

MUST I live here, with scripture on my walls,
    Death-cards with rocks and anchors; on my
    shelf
Plain men and women with plain histories
A proud landlady knows, and no one else?
Let me have pictures of a richer kind:
Scenes in low taverns, with their beggar rogues
Singing and drinking ale; who buy more joy
With a few pence than others can with pounds.
Show gipsies on wild commons, camped at fires
Close to their caravans; where they cook flesh
They have not bought, and plants not sold to them.
Show me the picture of a drinking monk
With his round belly like a mare in foal,
Belted, to keep his guts from falling out
When he laughs hearty; or a maid's bare back,
Who teases me with a bewitching smile
Thrown over her white shoulder. Let me see
The picture of a sleeping damosel,
Who has a stream of shining hair to fill

Up that deep channel banked by her white breasts.
Has Beauty never smiled from off these walls,
Has Genius never entered in a book?
Nay, Madam, keep your room ; for in my box
I have a lovely picture of young Eve,
Before she knew what sewing was. Alas:
If I hung on your wall her naked form,
Among your graves and crosses, scripture texts,
Your death-cards with their anchors and their
    rocks—
What then? I think this life a joyful thing,
And, like a bird that sees a sleeping cat,
I leave with haste your death-preparing room.

The Child and the Mariner

A DEAR old couple my grandparents were,
  And kind to all dumb things; they saw in
Heaven
The lamb that Jesus petted when a child;
Their faith was never draped by Doubt: to them
Death was a rainbow in Eternity,
That promised everlasting brightness soon.
An old seafaring man was he; a rough
Old man, but kind; and hairy, like the nut
Full of sweet milk.   All day on shore he watched
The winds for sailors' wives, and told what ships
Enjoyed fair weather, and what ships had storms;
He watched the sky, and he could tell for sure
What afternoons would follow stormy morns,
If quiet nights would end wild afternoons.
He leapt away from scandal with a roar,
And if a whisper still possessed his mind,
He walked about and cursed it for a plague.
He took offence at Heaven when beggars passed,
And sternly called them back to give them help.

In this old captain's house I lived, and things
That house contained were in ships' cabins once :
Sea-shells and charts and pebbles, model ships ;
Green weeds, dried fishes stuffed, and coral stalks ;
Old wooden trunks with handles of spliced rope,
With copper saucers full of monies strange,
That seemed the savings of dead men, not touched
To keep them warm since their real owners died ;
Strings of red beads, methought were dipped in
    blood,
And swinging lamps, as though the house might
    move ;
An ivory lighthouse built on ivory rocks,
The bones of fishes and three bottled ships.
And many a thing was there which sailors make
In idle hours, when on long voyages,
Of marvellous patience, to no lovely end.
And on those charts I saw the small black dots
That were called islands, and I knew they had
Turtles and palms, and pirates' buried gold.
There came a stranger to my granddad's house,
The old man's nephew, a seafarer too ;
A big, strong able man who could have walked
Twm Barlum's hill all clad in iron mail ;
So strong he could have made one man his club

90　The Child and the Mariner

To knock down others—Henry was his name,
No other name was uttered by his kin.
And here he was, insooth illclad, but oh,
Thought I, what secrets of the sea are his!
This man knows coral islands in the sea,
And dusky girls heartbroken for white men ;
This sailor knows of wondrous lands afar,
More rich than Spain, when the Phœnicians shipped
Silver for common ballast, and they saw
Horses at silver mangers eating grain ;
This man has seen the wind blow up a mermaid's
　　hair
Which, like a golden serpent, reared and stretched
To feel the air away beyond her head.
He begged my pennies, which I gave with joy—
He will most certainly return some time
A self-made king of some new land, and rich.
Alas that he, the hero of my dreams,
Should be his people's scorn ; for they had rose
To proud command of ships, whilst he had toiled
Before the mast for years, and well content ;
Him they despised, and only Death could bring
A likeness in his face to show like them.
For he drank all his pay, nor went to sea
As long as ale was easy got on shore.

Now, in his last long voyage he had sailed
From Plymouth Sound to where sweet odours fan
The Cingalese at work, and then back home—
But came not near his kin till pay was spent.
He was not old, yet seemed so; for his face
Looked like the drowned man's in the morgue,
    when it
Has struck the wooden wharves and keels of ships.
And all his flesh was pricked with Indian ink,
His body marked as rare and delicate
As dead men struck by lightning under trees,
And pictured with fine twigs and curlèd ferns;
Chains on his neck and anchors on his arms;
Rings on his fingers, bracelets on his wrist;
And on his breast the Jane of Appledore
Was schooner rigged, and in full sail at sea.
He could not whisper with his strong hoarse voice,
No more than could a horse creep quietly;
He laughed to scorn the men that muffled close
For fear of wind, till all their neck was hid,
Like Indian corn wrapped up in long green leaves;
He knew no flowers but seaweeds brown and green,
He knew no birds but those that followed ships.
Full well he knew the water-world; he heard
A grander music there than we on land,

92 The Child and the Mariner

When organ shakes a church; swore he would
    make
The sea his home, though it was always roused
By such wild storms as never leave Cape Horn;
Happy to hear the tempest grunt and squeal
Like pigs heard dying in a slaughterhouse.
A true-born mariner, and this his hope—
His coffin would be what his cradle was,
A boat to drown in and be sunk at sea;
To drown at sea and lie a dainty corpse
Salted and iced in Neptune's larder deep.
This man despised small coasters, fishing-smacks;
He scorned those sailors who at night and morn
Can see the coast, when in their little boats
They go a six days' voyage and are back
Home with their wives for every Sabbath day.
Much did he talk of tankards of old beer,
And bottled stuff he drank in other lands,
Which was a liquid fire like Hell to gulp,
But Paradise to sip.
           And so he talked;
Nor did those people listen with more awe
To Lazarus—whom they had seen stone dead—
Than did we urchins to that seaman's voice.
He many a tale of wonder told: of where,

At Argostoli, Cephalonia's sea
Ran over the earth's lip in heavy floods;
And then again of how the strange Chinese
Conversed much as our homely Blackbirds sing.
He told us how he sailed in one old ship
Near that volcano Martinique, whose power
Shook like dry leaves the whole Carribean seas;
And made the Sun set in a sea of fire
Which only half was his; and dust was thick
On deck, and stones were pelted at the mast.
So, as we walked along, that seaman dropped
Into my greedy ears such words that sleep
Stood at my pillow half the night perplexed.
He told how isles sprang up and sank again,
Between short voyages, to his amaze;
How they did come and go, and cheated charts;
Told how a crew was cursed when one man killed
A bird that perched upon a moving barque;
And how the sea's sharp needles, firm and strong,
Ripped open the bellies of big, iron ships;
Of mighty icebergs in the Northern seas,
That haunt the far horizon like white ghosts.
He told of waves that lift a ship so high
That birds could pass from starboard unto port
Under her dripping keel,

94 The Child and the Mariner

Oh, it was sweet

To hear that seaman tell such wondrous tales:
How deep the sea in parts, that drownèd men
Must go a long way to their graves and sink
Day after day, and wander with the tides.
He spake of his own deeds; of how he sailed
One summer's night along the Bosphorus,
And he—who knew no music like the wash
Of waves against a ship, or wind in shrouds—
Heard then the music on that woody shore
Of nightingales, and feared to leave the deck,
He thought 'twas sailing into Paradise.
To hear these stories all we urchins placed
Our pennies in that seaman's ready hand;
Until one morn he signed for a long cruise,
And sailed away—we never saw him more.
Could such a man sink in the sea unknown?
Nay, he had found a land with something rich,
That kept his eyes turned inland for his life.
" A damn bad sailor and a landshark too,
No good in port or out"—my granddad said.

THE END

Printed in the USA
CPSIA information can be obtained
at www.ICGtesting.com
LVHW011047271024
794927LV00035B/618